WRITING ESSAYS by PICTURES

a workbook

by Alke Gröppel-Wegener

Thank you to all the backers who supported the first version of this book through my Kickstarter campaign. - without your enthusiasm for the idea this extended version would never have happened!

Alke

Writing Essays by Pictures - A Workbook
Text: Alke Gröppel-Wegener
Design: Alke Gröppel-Wegener and Richard Mellor
www.tactileacademia.com

Paperback ISBN: 978-0-9576652-2-4

Published by Innovative Libraries, 2016.
195 Wakefield Road, Lepton, Huddersfield. HD8 0BL
andywalsh@innovativelibraries.org.uk
http://innovativelibraries.org.uk/

CONTENTS

You might have been attracted to this book because you dislike writing. The bad news is that you probably won't find a way to get out of the writing, and this book isn't about how to avoid writing at all costs. Really this book is about making the putting together of an evidence-based essay easier through understanding all the steps that should go into it - and writing is a part of this.

But, there are two pretty good strategies that make the writing easier:

The Bookworm Transformation
Reading for Fun

Become a Bookworm!

Yes you should be reading things for the essay itself, this is how you find most secondary research and this will be covered starting from page 12, but one of the best ways to become a better writer is to read things that you enjoy reading. And yes, that includes fiction. Or non-fiction. Whatever you like to read! As long as what you read has been written by professional writers (which means that it has been worked on for a long time and revised and edited to make it even better) this will improve both your spelling and your grammar. It is a good way to get rid of the fear of the written word. If you don't like to read, maybe because you are dyslexic, try audio books. They won't do much for your spelling, but they can potentially foster an appreciation of words as story-telling devices and do wonders for your grammar.

Write Little, Write Often!

The other strategy to make writing easier is to do a little bit at a time, but do it often. Instead of panicking about it for the whole of the term and then being forced to write everything in one go, break that mammoth task into   little tasks and get on with one at a time.

You could see this as the 'snacking approach' to writing. Instead of going through everything that you need to do in one single sitting, much like a Christmas dinner or similar, you should spread out your 'calorie intake' to have a little here and a little there. Taking your time allows you to sample more, to think about it more (in effect digesting it more fully) and also to practise it more.

But equally this is very much like construction - don't think of it as a wall that you bang your head against, rather focus on the bricks that make up that wall - and assemble your wall one brick at a time.

This Assembly Approach to Writing is really what is behind the idea of this workbook. Here you can explore the stages that go into researching and writing an essay from a number of perspectives.

All these sections use visual metaphors and analogies which are designed to highlight specific, important aspects of academia.

NOT ALL OF THE VISUAL ANALOGIES MIGHT APPEAL TO YOU, FEEL FREE TO BE SELECTIVE, USE WHAT MAKES SENSE TO YOU!

In order to get you into the habit of doing a little, but doing it often, most sections also include something for you to do. Sometimes that is something you can complete in the book itself, sometimes something to keep in envelopes inside, and sometimes (particularly towards the end) it is something to include in your next essay draft.

(And yes, there should be more than one draft! Just like anything else, essay writing is something that needs to be practised. That's why a lot of things here are for you to try out, little projects to get you working on this regularly, because the more you work on it, the better it will get - one brick at a time.)

So let's get started...

Here's the trouble with writing academic essays at degree level:

> if you haven't been to university before, you probably haven't done it before.

You will have written all sorts of things:

letters, emails, short stories, social media up-dates, txts, reports, blog posts,

and much much more.

You might even have written essays, but if you haven't been to uni before, you probably haven't been writing the sort of essays that university lecturers are looking for. And this might be a problem, because when they say 'essay' you hear 'essay' - but you are both talking about different things.

Because quite a lot of what makes up an **academic** essay is specifically academic practice: using research to rigorously back up your argument, including evidence to back up your points - and even writing it to a specific blueprint.

To make matters worse, some of this practice is 'hidden', - academics do it, but it has become such second nature to them that they forget how to explain that they are doing it (and how they are doing it).

An essay ● might seem like a straight line when you are reading it, ●

but ● really ● it ● paints ● a ● picture ● for ● the ● reader ● ● ●

a ● bit ● like ● a ●

● ● connect - the - dots ● ● ● drawing ● ● ●

The ● further ● you ● read, the ● more ● defined it ● becomes,

● ● ● and ● once ● you ● are ● finished ● you ● can ● see ● the ● whole ● picture.

Unveiling Hidden Academic Practice

When you are writing an essay this is a bit like the planning of a connect-the-dots drawing. Only because this is research you don't make up the image, you first find it within the evidence you consult. That means you first have to identify lots of evidence you could use, because you have to find a lot of possible points. While you are doing that you might go round and round in circles and squiggly lines, there is no real order yet, you are exploring at this stage.

Then you go through a process of 'curation' - you figure out what your argument is and what points you need in order to make it. This will mean looking at all the dots you have and getting rid of the ones that don't fit into your picture.

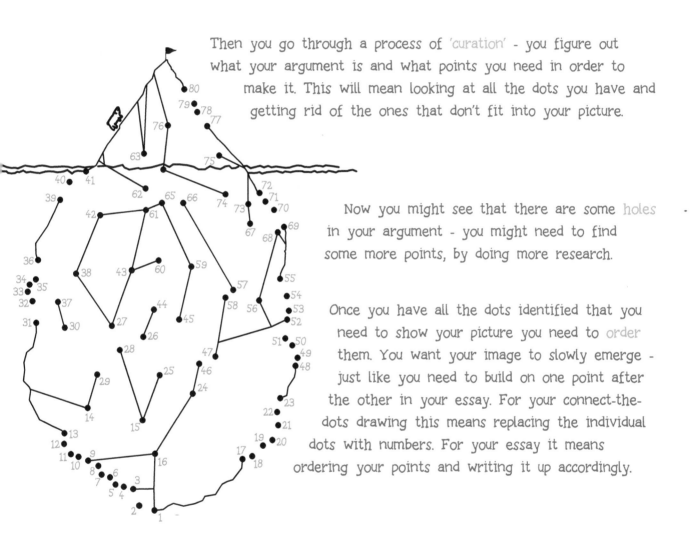

Now you might see that there are some holes in your argument - you might need to find some more points, by doing more research.

Once you have all the dots identified that you need to show your picture you need to order them. You want your image to slowly emerge - just like you need to build on one point after the other in your essay. For your connect-the-dots drawing this means replacing the individual dots with numbers. For your essay it means ordering your points and writing it up accordingly.

So you as writer (and really researcher) find the evidence, identify the argument and then present it in a way that it effortlessly appears to the reader.

All the stages that go into this planning process of researching and writing an essay are hidden from the reader. But for the essay to work the writer needs to go through them.

This workbook is all about getting you to understand this 'hidden' academic practice - in a hands-on way.

The problem with first essays students produce
is very often that they are not very 'deep'
– they are not focused enough. In a way they could be described
as ice sheets floating on the academic ocean

little flat bits of research over the waterline (the actual essay you see) and very little research backing it up (the bits under the waterline).

Frequently these are more like descriptive lists, one thing is mentioned after the other, but they are not necessarily linked in any way beyond an initial theme. For a reader (imagine a polar bear exploring your ice sheet), this could be seen as two things

somewhat boring (it's a flat piece of ice, after all), and also potentially dangerous,

as it is so thin the ice sheet may capsize once the bear gets to its edge.

You don't want to bore your readers or drown them in the confusion an insufficiently backed up argument can lead to.

Building Research

In order for you to keep your readers safe (and interested),
what you need to do is model your essay and research process
on an iceberg,   not an ice sheet.

The
iceberg
comes to a point,
challenging your
polar bear and providing
some interest, just like your
essay should have one main focus,
one specific argument you want to make.

If you want a 'grounded' argument

(and in an academic essay you do!),

there needs to be a large chunk of research

backing it up,

sitting under the waterline,

much bigger, in fact, than the actual essay itself.

Doing this research allows you to explore 'academic depth'

much more than if you were

writing something based on

'shallow research.

The Spotlight Specification
Finding Focus

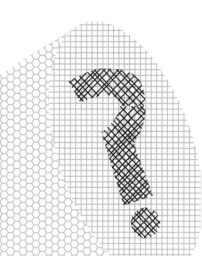

Before you dive into the waters of
academia to begin your research, there
is one thing you have to do first –
and it is a very important step
indeed:
you need to figure out
your focus.

Without knowing your focus, you won't know what to research.
If you don't know what to research you won't find any good
sources; and without good sources, you won't be able to back
up your argument with evidence… you'll end up with information
that is too general and won't be able to identify the picture
you want to emerge for your reader. Even if you are working
on an extremely long piece of work, you will not be able to
write a history of everything. You need a specific subject,
something that will take centre stage in your spotlight.

Of course if you are required to research and write for university,
you might have a really specific question to answer (as set by your
lecturer). More likely, however, is it that the question has some
room for interpretation or that you have to come up with your own
question.

This can be quite scary! But it is also a great opportunity because
it means that you can find an angle that you are really interested
in. The more you are interested, the more fun it will be, the more
research you will do, the better grounded your writing will be, the
better the work will be.

(And the great thing about having a question is that you'll know
you're done when you can answer it!)

CREATE A POSTCARD THAT REPRESENTS YOUR FOCUS.

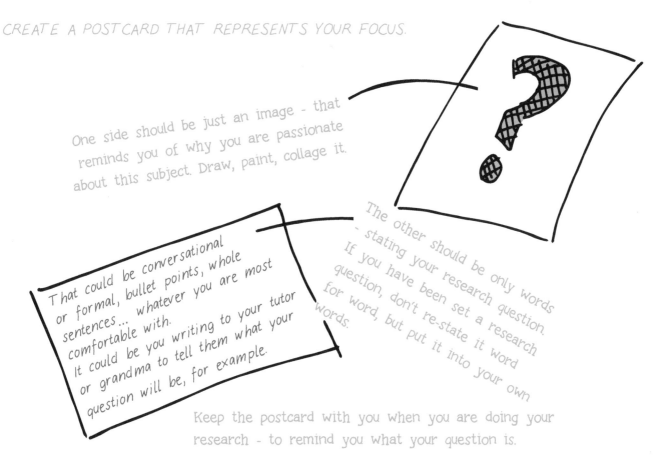

One side should be just an image - that reminds you of why you are passionate about this subject. Draw, paint, collage it.

The other should be only words - stating your research question. If you have been set a research question, don't re-state it word for word, but put it into your own words.

That could be conversational or formal, bullet points, whole sentences... whatever you are most comfortable with.
It could be you writing to your tutor or grandma to tell them what your question will be, for example.

Keep the postcard with you when you are doing your research - to remind you what your question is.

Cut slits into this page (be careful not to cut the one below) and you can slot your postcard in here when you don't need it.

Tying down your focus makes it much clearer for you to follow, which is a great help when avoiding a sneaky research trap: tangential procrastination.
The postcard should remind you of your starting point... and hopefully help you avoid going off on a tangent of researching stuff that is quite interesting, but not actually connected to your research question, an indirect waste of time to be avoided at all cost!

P.S.: you might come across a shift in your research while you are doing it and decide to change your research focus - that is fair enough, just make a new postcard. (Although be careful to not do this too often...)

Academic research needs to be evidence based.

Like solving a murder (where you also have very specific questions - Who did it? How? And Why?), you can't just go with your gut feeling. What if you get it wrong and the wrong person gets convicted?

Everything you put in your academic research you need to be able to back up by evidence. For that we use two kinds of sources: primary and secondary.

Primary sources are when you look at data yourself. Like observing the murder scene. How did the body fall? Where did the blood flow? In the academic context your observations might come from a visit to a museum, looking at a film or analysing a book. Primary sources are often 'stuff' - things you observe yourself.

Secondary sources are what other people have found out about the 'stuff'. Like reports about the evidence collected at a crime scene that has been analysed by experts, who in this report tell you what it means. Very often these get published in books or as articles, but you can also find them in interviews or documentaries, for example.

Before we get into nifty ways of taking notes (from both primary and secondary sources) and how to find out if a secondary source is a good one, there is another important thing to keep in mind:

Just like if you were a police detective, when you're working on a research project, you are working on a case of sorts - and in order for all the evidence to be admissible you have to keep track of where it comes from.

In academic terms this is called **referencing**. Basically this means that you give your readers enough information about your sources that they could go and find the sources themselves. In academia there are a number of different referencing systems, and it is really important to find out from your tutors which one you are supposed to use – this could be different from subject to subject (so you might not use the same system as your friend who is studying something else), or even from tutor to tutor (so you might have to use different ones for different essays).

The referencing systems usually have two parts: something you put **into the text** to show that here is information you found somewhere else (this could be a footnote or something in brackets for example), and then the full information in a **reference list** or **bibliography**.

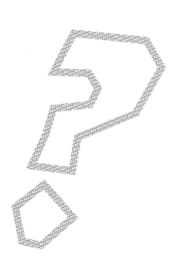

Think of it as an address, every source you find 'lives' somewhere and you need to give this address to your readers, so you include a full address book at the end and in the text you put little shortcuts so that your reader can find the full address easily.

Warning:

Very often lecturers use the terms 'bibliography' and 'reference list' interchangeably. Technically a reference list includes only the sources you have actually referred to in your writing, a bibliography can also include sources that you came across in your research that were important for developing your thinking, but that you ended up not citing. If you are in doubt what your lecturers want, ask them to clarify!

The referencing is really important, because if you don't put it in, you don't give the people who put all the work into the source in the first place the credit they deserve. In academic terms this is considered fraud (also called plagiarism) and it is taken very seriously. On the other hand, a full bibliography shows that you have done lots of research, you should show that (and then get credit for it).

START YOUR OWN SOURCES ADDRESSBOOK OR CASEFILE.

First: find out the **referencing system** you are supposed to use. Note down

1.   what information you need for this (Author's name? Year of publication? Title?, etc.)

2.   what order you need it in

3.   if there is any formatting that is important (do you have to put some things in italics or bold?)

Find out examples of the types of sources you are likely to need (for example Book, Journal Article, Website, Film, etc.) and write them here:

_____

_____

_____

_____

Find out how the **in-text citation** works for your referencing system - are you supposed to include something in the text? Should you be working with foot- or endnotes? Note it down here:

_____

_____

Lastly find out how to **order** this information in the bibliography for your essay - is it alphabetically? in order of appearance? something else?

_____

_____

Use this space to start your own bibliography.

Once you know what your focus is going to be (or maybe even on the way to establishing your focus), you will need to collect information that will help you construct your argument. This is some of the bulk of the 'Underwater Iceberg', and you will need to sift through a lot of information until you can whittle it down to the bits you actually need. Now that you know how to reference your sources, you need to put a system in place to take notes effectively – effectively for you, that is.

There are a number of ways of documenting information, for example through written notes or collecting documentary photographic evidence like the snapshot, but **taking notes should go beyond the documenting stage**. Good working with notes includes leaving spaces for your own thoughts and links to put different sources and issues into context with each other. This is what makes notes useful, and the best way of taking them is to get your 'visual brain' in on the act. Useful ways to do this include collage and documentary drawing.

The Cut and Paste Philosophy
Collaging Notes

Starting points **for your research occur all over your time at university:**

lectures,

seminars or

workshops

are full of things to find out more about.

But this is a very special kind of research, because it is full of ready-made information provided by your teachers. Great first steps, but keep in mind that this is almost **pre-digested** - somebody else has selected sources for you and then probably also interpreted them (or helped you interpret them yourself).

The challenge here is not to rely on this too much (after all it isn't your actual research), but to find a way to make this your own, to turn it into starting points for your own research.

You should always prepare for a teaching session and go through your notes afterwards, and here is a nifty way of taking notes that allows you to make them as personal for yourself as possible:

A reflective book can be a very simple book structure,

such as a long strip of paper folded into an accordion,

that you use to take notes and reflect visually. This can be a really good way to take notes that are meaningful for you - rather than merely copying information (lecture slides, for example, you will probably be able to get access to directly anyway, so there is no real point in copying them. However, you might use the slides as a starting point for some collaging.)

So, grab something from your paper recycling pile and start collaging and taking visual notes.

The important thing here is NOT to try and replicate the information presented to you, be that in lecture or book form, as pod-cast or film, radio programme or website, but rather to let your mind wander and allow it to make connections to your own work and understanding.

You might find images or words,
or make your own.
As this is your personal note-taking,
there is no wrong way - anything goes!

The great thing to get started with collage is that it is 'only' ripping
and cutting, sticking and pasting, you need very little equipment,
and pretty much anybody can do it, even if you
are not feeling artistic, *give it a go!*

Use collage to take notes during an event (maybe a lecture?) making a short reflective book and keep it in the envelope overleaf

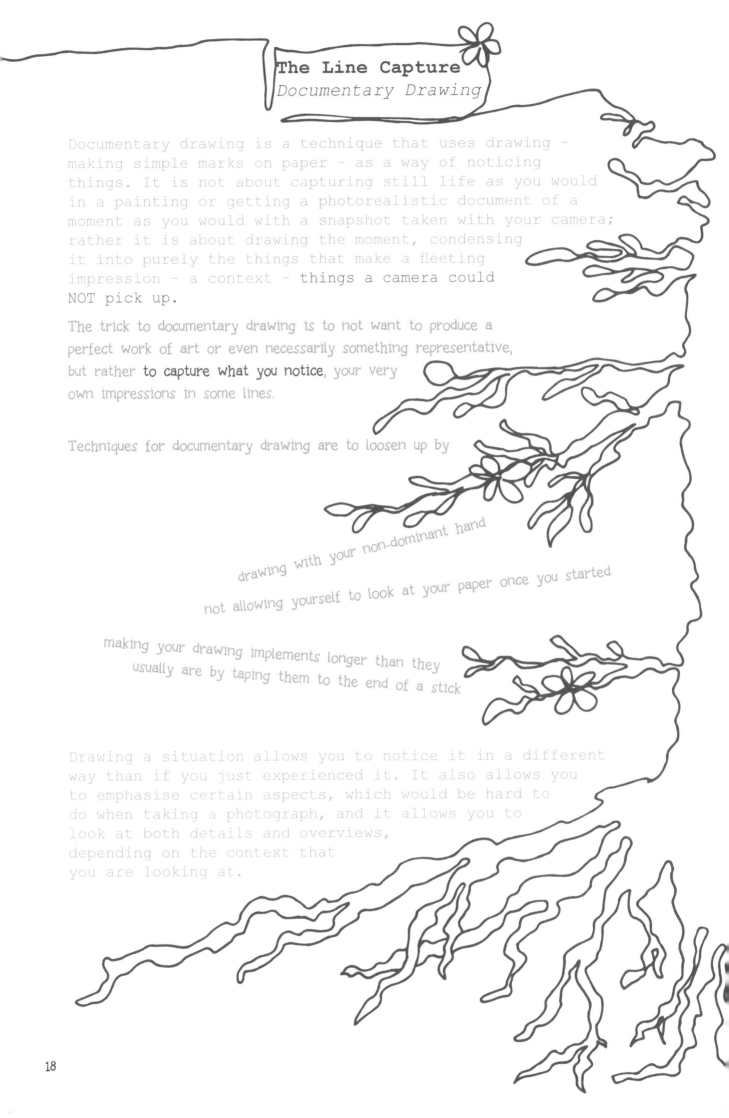

The Line Capture
Documentary Drawing

Documentary drawing is a technique that uses drawing –
making simple marks on paper – as a way of noticing
things. It is not about capturing still life as you would
in a painting or getting a photorealistic document of a
moment as you would with a snapshot taken with your camera;
rather it is about drawing the moment, condensing
it into purely the things that make a fleeting
impression – a context – things a camera could
NOT pick up.

The trick to documentary drawing is to not want to produce a
perfect work of art or even necessarily something representative,
but rather **to capture what you notice**, your very
own impressions in some lines.

Techniques for documentary drawing are to loosen up by

drawing with your non-dominant hand

not allowing yourself to look at your paper once you started

making your drawing implements longer than they
usually are by taping them to the end of a stick

Drawing a situation allows you to notice it in a different
way than if you just experienced it. It also allows you
to emphasise certain aspects, which would be hard to
do when taking a photograph, and it allows you to
look at both details and overviews,
depending on the context that
you are looking at.

Try this out by documenting what's on your desk right now in here

Then take it further:

    Use fast sketches to document a museum visit or film.

    Only take notes in images that you draw yourself.

    Use found materials as background of your drawings,

                    for example train tickets or paper bags.

GLUE IN AN ENVELOPE HERE TO KEEP YOUR VISUAL NOTES IN

It is important to realise that when you are engaged in visual note-taking, the images themselves (and particularly the quality of the images) aren't the important thing - it is about the thoughts and ideas these visuals trigger in you. Therefore these visual notes will never really be transferable, i.e. if somebody else looks at them, they will probably not be able to understand what you were trying to say (whereas if you are writing in full or partial sentences, you would expect other people to be able to take up your notes without a problem).

In true note-taking style, the important bit is not actually taking the initial notes; it is what you do with your notes that counts. So the next step is crucial: turning the impressions you captured into fully formed thoughts and knowledge that you can express in words.

With visual notes that means that you need to take time to interpret what you have made, allowing time to reflect on the information - and giving you the opportunity to put this information into your own specific context! You could do this by talking through it with somebody (a 'critical friend') or you could write a narrative about it, telling your reader the story of the images you found and selected, and why they are significant.

This is a bit like looking at your notes as a whole and deciding which information to

'zoom' in on.

You need to ask yourself which details to 'frame' and which to ignore..

Is there a particular issue that is especially important? This needs to be singled out and discussed in detail.

Maybe there are a number of aspects that could be framed which show similar things or deal with similar issues, - these could be seen or described as a sequence belonging together, like a number of paintings from the same series.

But also think about the level of detail, because some things make more sense if you look at them very closely, while others need a mid- or long-shot (to use film speak).

In other words, some things make sense when looking at them like

an overview,

others in

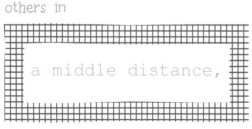
a middle distance,

others still as

a detail.

The process of 'sorting' your notes in this way is the first step of analysing them. Now you can start to turn them from images, which might only make sense to you, into words that are shareable.

The easiest way for a lot of people of taking that step is to have a conversation with somebody, a trusted person or 'critical' friend. This should be somebody that you can trust not to make fun of your artwork (as we know it isn't actually about the artwork, it is about the ideas). It is amazing how much easier it is to talk about a collage or a drawing than it is to try to put ideas in your head directly into written words.

You can also write down an imagined conversation, for example you could pretend you're in the pub talking to a friend. This is often easier than facing a blank piece of paper or computer screen trying to write an academic piece of work. It might be helpful to record it first and then transcribe it to get the first words down.

Having identified the different frames that are important is a really helpful preparation process for this, as it is an initial step in prioritising and analysing the data you have collected (and yes, your notes should be counted as data!)

Use the visual documents you have created, be it collage, (documentary) drawing or maybe a combination of the two, and analysed through the framing exercise, use this frame to start writing them up as notes that are shareable. At this point don't worry about making this sound formal, or spelling or grammar, just put together a document (which could also include images, really the frames you have identified) that is a shareable version of the notes you took.

Once you have filled this frame, make your own notes and add to the envelope on the previous page.

While using collage and drawing are particularly useful when investigating primary sources, i.e. stuff, they might not be that useful when dealing with text. Future sections will be looking at ways that you can use to look at and work with text particularly, but first we have to figure out how to find good texts for your research.

Although people often talk about the 'information landscape', it is actually very difficult to see landmarks that rise like mountain tops when you are immersed in research. It can feel more like a seemingly endless ocean of information and it can be very difficult to figure out what exactly goes on below the surface.

The Ocean of Literature
Finding sources

Let's think of sources as sea creatures living in this ocean of literature. In order to find the ones useful to us, we need to first explore the ocean

In the beginning stages of your research, keep it shallow. Skim read and look for general sources.

What you need to do

It is important to have a good idea of what your focus is, what you need to research, what you need to discard as interesting, but not relevant. So always have your focus postcard on hand when you are searching for sources.

The most obvious way to search for information these days is to surf. Websurfing, just like surfing the waves on the ocean, allows you to skim along on the surface of the information: that way you cover a lot of ground, but not in-depth.

Cast your net wide, but keep track of your search terms or keywords.

Notice where you are finding information that seems promising.

Keep in mind that subject disciplines outside of your own area might also have information on your topic, which might come in handy.

at this stage is map the ocean for promising fishing grounds

Draw a map of different 'oceans' of literature you might want to tap into (start with key words or databases) and populate them with sources as you go along. Which are fish rich, i.e. full of promising sources? Which aren't? Are there authors who seem popular?

Your map will help you keep track of how useful certain key words are, and which areas to tap into once you go 'deeper' in your academic search

That is perfect for this stage, but you need to be careful you don't unleash a tsunami of information under which you can drown

ADD TO YOUR MAP AS YOUR RESEARCH CONTINUES

Now that you know where the fish-rich areas are, you need to start thinking about what kind of sea creatures you can find.

While information these days seems to be everywhere, this doesn't necessarily make research easier. On the contrary, in some ways it makes it harder, because you don't just have to find **any** information, you have to find the **right kind** of information.

Keep in mind that what gets spewed out by a search engine is like the contents of the net of a trawler - there can be all kinds of sea creatures in it.

The content you find on the web is predetermined by the keywords you search for. However, the results are usually ordered by popularity, rather than the criteria you need as an academic researcher.

The Fishscale of Academicness

Try to think of each individual source and what it would look like if it was a sea creature - and why?

Would it be curled up, because the information is presented in a roundabout way?

Would it be fat, because it gives you a lot of information on a very specific topic?

Would it be bright and friendly, because it has lots of pictures in it and is easy to understand?

Would it be straight, because the information is presented in a clear way, possibly chronologically?

This means that you have to make your own decision as to whether the source is any good for your context – and for that you have to not just pay attention to the **content**, but also to the **type** of source you have found!

Ask yourself:

Has it been written by an expert?

Is it reliable?

What audience has it been written for?

There are different types of sources and some of them you should really not use as academic evidence, because they may be biased, too simplistic or plain wrong.

Whenever you are backing up your argument with literature, this should be in your mind – and if you are marked on the piece in question, the quality of the sources you use will be taken into account.

Evaluating Sources

Try to do this without thinking of the content, just of the type of source it is!

Would it be grey and with dangerous teeth, because it has no illustrations and uses unfamiliar words?

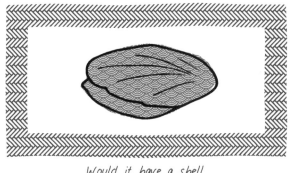

Would it have a shell, because it is hard to get into?

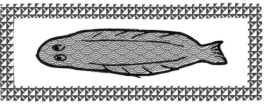

Would it be flat, because it mentions a lot of areas, but none of them in any depth?

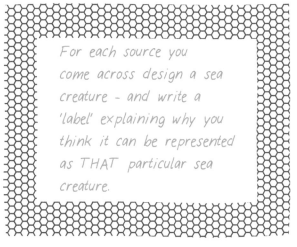

For each source you come across design a sea creature - and write a 'label' explaining why you think it can be represented as THAT particular sea creature.

Now that you know what types of sources you are dealing with,
think about at what depth they live
in the academic ocean:

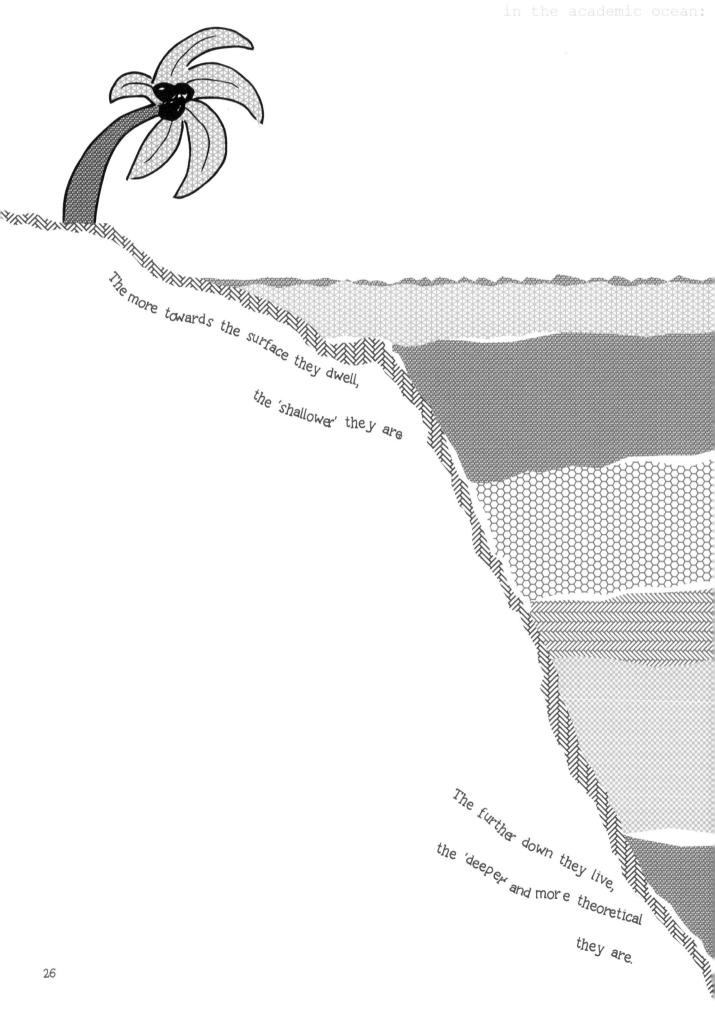

The more towards the surface they dwell,

the 'shallower' they are

The further down they live,

the 'deeper' and more theoretical

they are.

Children's books are friendly, in bold colours, and roam very much towards the surface.

Personal opinion pieces, such as blog posts, reviews or letters to the editor, are usually just that: personal.

That means they are less academic, because they are subjective - even if they are written by experts. Like goldfish they are little gems, but not really that substantial.

They also tend to be short and not linked, like one in a swarm of little fish.

Newspaper articles are a good example of texts written for a general audience. If published in a reputable newspaper they are researched well, but they might show some bias.

They make far reaching links and put their subjects into a larger context, but usually stop short of real academic depth as they are aimed at non-experts.

Academic journal articles tend to be grouped around the theme of the journal, or possibly even a special issue. Reading them can be quite daunting, because basically they are written by experts for experts.

If a journal is peer-reviewed that is a sign of academic depth, because here it is experts that decide (sometimes reading 'blind' so not knowing who authored a paper) what goes in the journal. These sources definitely have teeth - we could see them as sharks or piranha, or we could imagine them with a shell that is difficult to get into.

Introductory academic texts, like Readers, are a good starting point, because they will get you familiar with the key ideas and debates in the field, its jargon and probably also introduce notable authors.

They tend to be 'flat' in that they usually cover only an overview of a field of work, possibly not going into detail.

They can also take the form of a quite linear narrative, for example showing a chronological order of events `one bit happening after the other.

You might also come across texts that are just too weird. They might have developed at too deep a level to make sense to a non-expert. As you put in more work in the years to come, you might build up the skills to dive deeper and understand them more easily. .

However, some might always remain out of reach, unless you are doing a PhD in a very related area.

Once you have identified your sources (and what type of sea creature they are), here is some advice on how to deal with them:

Ask yourself whether the sources you have found are shallow or deep (in terms of 'academicness')? Consider who they were written by (a professor? a professional? a fan?), what audience they were written for (children? adults? students? experts?), their writing style (formal? informal?), and also look out for clues of academic writing.

These clues are hidden in the academic conventions. Most important is to look out for **bibliographies** - sources that tell us where their evidence comes from are very promising (and useful, see below).

Other clues are **foot-** or **end-notes** - a way to add extra information to a text, **indexes** - a sort of contents page full of key words at the back of a book, **appendices** - extra information in the back of a book or report, **glossaries** - lists of explanations of the technical terms used -, as well as **abstracts** - little summaries of the research at the beginning of an article.

Really at the beginning the trick is to find just one source that is at an appropriate academic level and has the right sort of content. Because then you can 'explode' your literature seach by using the sources it uses. This is where bibliographies come in really handy.

Exploding a Literature Search

Remember that on page 13 a bibliography was likened to an address book? Once you find a good source in your area you can 'borrow' its address book to find more sources. Carefully read the bibliography and look for titles that sound related to what you are looking for - and then try to access them through your library. Also look for authors that have published things that sound relevant - and not only try to find the sources listed, but also see if those authors have written other things that relates to your research (maybe you can find something really recent or even get in touch with that author).

So while it might take some time to find your first academic source, once you have it this can help you find many, many more that are on the same level!

Academic texts can be quite substantial and they can be quite a slow read – particularly if you are not used to reading at this level of depth. There are a number of ways you can deal with this (and you can find some ways to do this on the next pages), but the most important is probably to keep in mind that you don't have to tackle a whole book or article in one sitting: rather you could break it up into sections and summarise them in your own words – breaking down a big scary source into smaller, more easily digestible sea creatures…

Overall, academic texts should be challenging. They have teeth, which means that there should be a bit of a struggle – reading them is hard work! – and getting to grips with them will be worth it in the end, because they contain good evidence.

However, you shouldn't get frustrated by them: if you have given it a go, carefully re-reading sections and looking up words that you don't understand, maybe they do live out of your depth for now. Swim back up to find some introductory sources, which should help you establish the ideas, debates and perspectives and get you familiar with the jargon, and maybe later in your academic career you can dive back down, when tackling a source in the deepest academic abyss will have become easier.

Take your sea creature designs and rank them according to their 'academicness'.

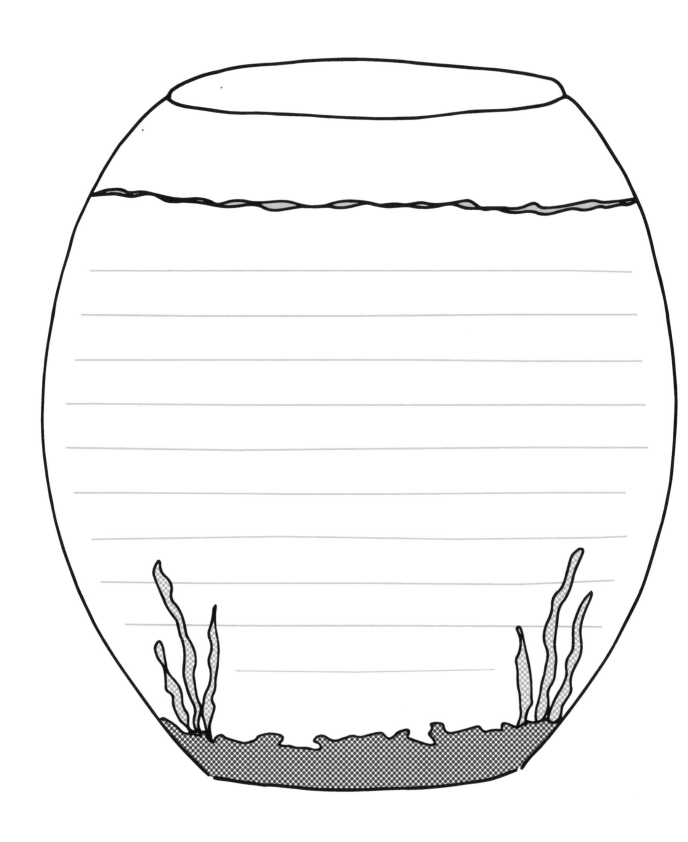

Now ask yourself: are they at the appropriate depth for your research?

BEWARE OF SOURCES THAT ARE TOO SHALLOW FOR YOUR LEVEL!

Now that you have your sources identified, it is all about making the most of them.

The Map Organisation
Working with Text

Reading a text, especially at this level, is not really like the reading you come across in everyday life. Reading an academic journal article will take longer than reading an article in a magazine. Reading a book chapter in an academic book will take longer than reading a chapter of a novel. The sentences will probably be longer, some of the words might be unfamiliar, and you need to question the claims made. You should also take notes.

So academic reading isn't quite like other reading. You can think of this difference like of the difference between a map describing a journey and the documentation of the actual journey

between a map

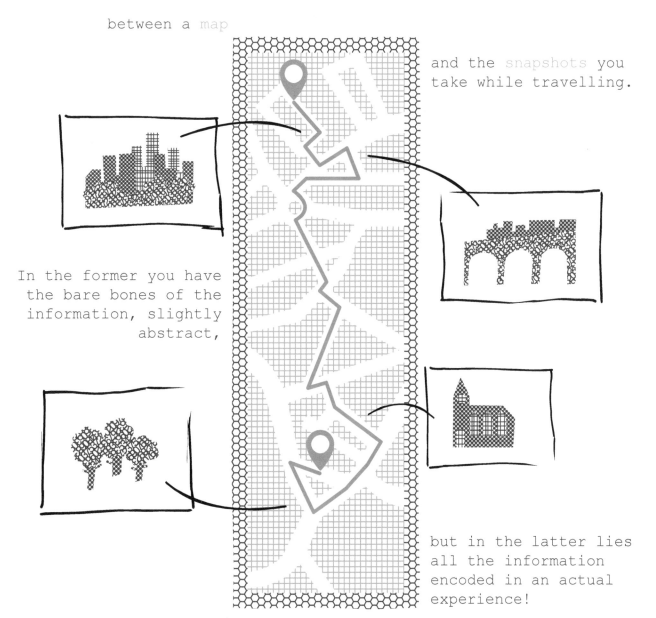

and the snapshots you take while travelling.

In the former you have the bare bones of the information, slightly abstract,

but in the latter lies all the information encoded in an actual experience!

Let's experience this by taking a 'long short walk'.
Use this space to draw a map of a walk that usually takes you 5 minutes.

This is a bit like simply reading - you check off every word and get from A to B, but are not really taking in a deeper meaning, asking yourself what is really going on in the text.

Now walk that 5 minute walk, but take 20 minutes. Use this space to map your walk. Document the journey by really noticing what is happening, what you can see, hear, smell, taste, feel...

See how much more detailed your map has become with these annotations? When you are reading at degree level, your reading should be like the long short walk, not like the purposeful stride where you don't really pay attention.

Reading at this level means really engaging with a text, rather than just skimming it once from the first to the last word. Really try to notice the text – what is the author trying to say? What does this mean in relation to the other texts you have read? What does this mean in relation to all the other sources which were not text based that you have come across? Does it give you ideas as to other issues you might want to look at? These are all things you need to be aware of, and might want to note down!

A good way to get used to working with text is to use a research strategy called 'poetic inquiry'.

The key idea behind this is that you go through a text and let words and phrases within it inspire you to condense it into a summary in form of a poem (don't worry, you don't need to get it to rhyme).

This sounds a bit abstract until you actually GIVE IT A GO:

Use a print-out or photocopy of an academic text and use scissors to literally take it apart. Cut out words or phrases that you find most meaningful. Now, puzzle them back together in a new order so that they represent how this particular text makes sense to you personally.
Stick them down in that order here

Give it a name

Just like with the collaging and documentary drawing this is only the first step. A good next step is to write an interpretation of your poem, and only then go back to the original text, maybe discussing it with a larger group - it can be really interesting to see which phrases are used by a number of people, and which are specific to you.

Glue in an envelope here to keep a copy of your original text in

Write a short text interpreting your poem

Then write up your notes/interpretation of the original text

Keep them all in the envelope.

Now that you have practiced noticing and interpreting texts, you are in the realm of organising the information that you got from the sources you found and reviewing that literature.

You should put together an overview of each source you might want to use in your research, which isn't a summary of the whole source, but only the bits that are important to your focus – you are 'condensing' the source by discarding the unimportant bits. This is called an **annotated bibliography** and on some courses you might be asked to do this as part of your assignment.

For each source, make a 'greeting card' that reminds you of this text:

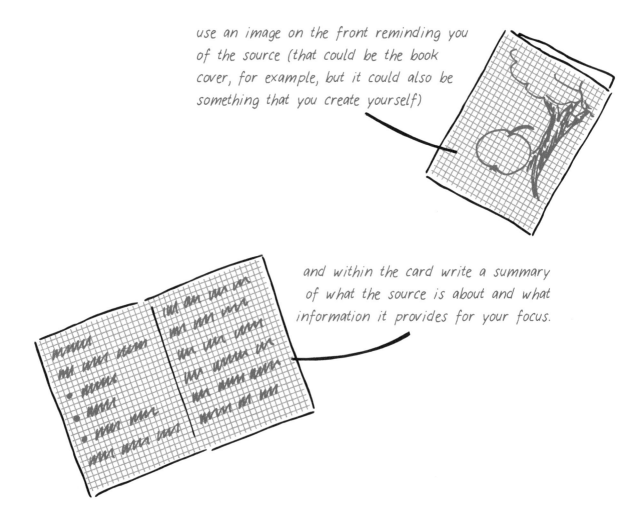

use an image on the front reminding you of the source (that could be the book cover, for example, but it could also be something that you create yourself)

and within the card write a summary of what the source is about and what information it provides for your focus.

Annotating Literature

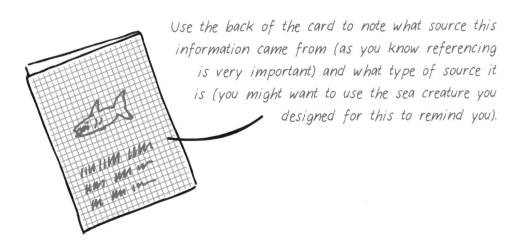

Use the back of the card to note what source this information came from (as you know referencing is very important) and what type of source it is (you might want to use the sea creature you designed for this to remind you).

Why would you want to do this? Well, the first time you introduce a source in an essay, you should really explain what type of source it is and who it is by (more on that on page 52). If you have made a greeting card you have an easy way of identifying this information, even if you are writing your essay in a few months' time, the image and information in this card will allow you to recall the important bits.

Based on the greeting cards you made of each of your sources, write an annotated bibliography, i.e. a list of all the sources and your 'review' of why each of them is useful or not in your context.

Glue an envelope here and keep your cards in it.

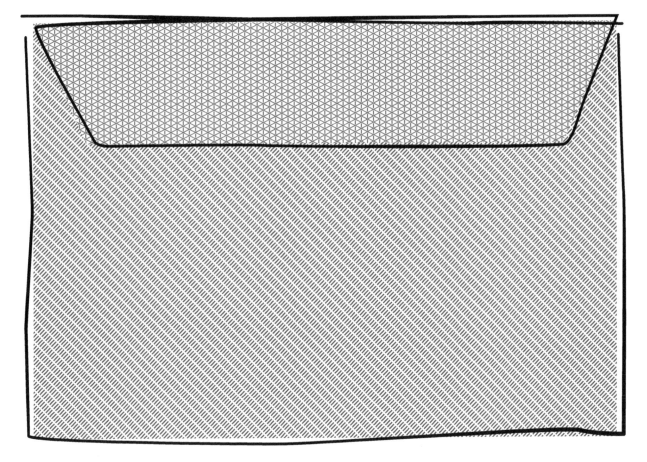

Now that you have a way of reminding yourself of the sources, it is time to specifically look at the content. One way of making sure your research doesn't lose focus is to physically condense your notes on sources to just what is relevant for the subject you are looking at. So instead of keeping the whole source (that book probably needs to be returned to the library anyway), only concentrate on the 'bits' you find interesting for your context.

However, it can be quite difficult to 'let go' of the source, because it is ordered in a way that makes sense. But neither all the information nor the order might be relevant in the context of your research. And your readers are less interested in a summary of the sources you use than in what you have actually found out. While they want you to present relevant information – and tell them where you found that – it needs to be tailored to your own context. For your reader it shows more of your understanding of the issues and debates if you put them into context with one another.

In other words, you need to 'free' the information, issues and debates from the order the author put them in, because what the original author found important might not be what is most important in your context.

Imagine all the information in the sources you want to use like playing cards in a brand new pack. Every source is represented by a different suit of cards. You can't keep hold of all of the cards, because that is too much information. So you need to discard some of them - those that are not connected to your focus.

Maybe you need only even numbers,

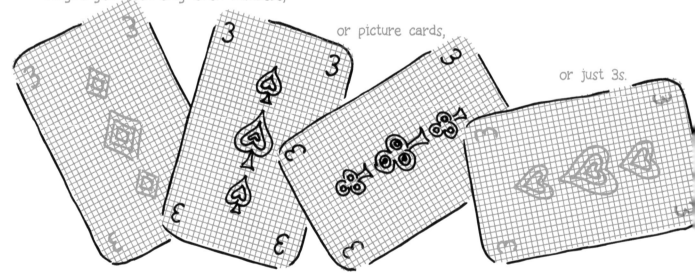

or picture cards,

or just 3s.

Break up the information in your sources by creating postcards with the specific content that you might want to use in your research. For each greeting card you are now making a series of postcards representing this content. These might be word-for-word quotations, summaries in your own words as well as your own thoughts and questions.
Use one card for each issue or idea.

Reviewing Literature

Here's a good way of dealing with word-for-word quotations:

 copy them down exactly! If something is in italics, bold or underlined, make sure you do the same in your notes.

 enclose them in quotation marks. Use either double quotation marks (") or single ones (') - you might be required to use one or the other for your actual essay, but for now it doesn't matter. But be consistent (it is always good practice to be consistent)

 always take note of the page number (if there is one) where you found the quote - you will need this information later

Mark the cards belonging together, so that you know which one came from which source and corresponds to each of the greeting cards you made. You could number them or give each source its own little icon which is repeated on each of the cards coming from that source.

 It is also a good idea to use a different colour for your own thoughts - so that you are able to tell later which thoughts were yours, and which came from the author.

You could include images if you think they will be helpful to you.

Now that you have condensed a whole stack of research materials to only the bits that are important for your current research, you can **get rid of the original source!** Return that book to the library, file (or recycle) that printed out article, click away from the website.

Separating the information out this way allows you to do something crucial: it has just become easier to order your information according to the issues. Rather than discussing the information you have found based on the order in the sources you found it in, you can now order them so that you can discuss it based on separate issues – thinking back to the playing cards, you can now put (and discuss) all the 3s together and then move on to the queens, and so on.

This helps you to produce a **Literature Review**. Here you not only present the relevant information from the sources that you have found, but you also put it into context with each other, analyse and compare it – based on the issues rather than where it came from (although you of course do need to reference it properly).

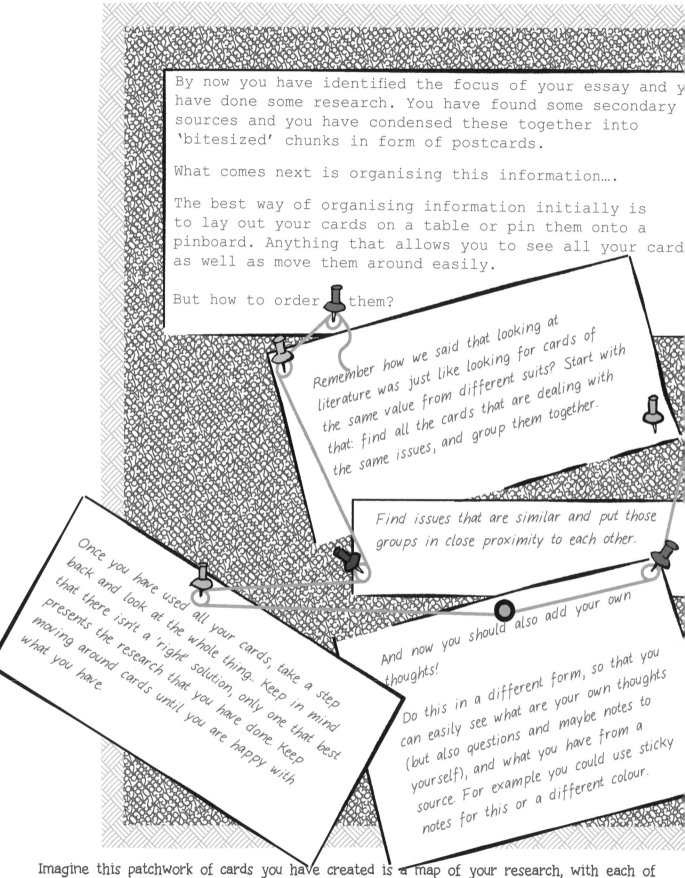

By now you have identified the focus of your essay and y
have done some research. You have found some secondary
sources and you have condensed these together into
'bitesized' chunks in form of postcards.

What comes next is organising this information....

The best way of organising information initially is
to lay out your cards on a table or pin them onto a
pinboard. Anything that allows you to see all your card
as well as move them around easily.

But how to order them?

Remember how we said that looking at literature was just like looking for cards of the same value from different suits? Start with that: find all the cards that are dealing with the same issues, and group them together.

Find issues that are similar and put those groups in close proximity to each other.

And now you should also add your own thoughts!

Do this in a different form, so that you can easily see what are your own thoughts (but also questions and maybe notes to yourself), and what you have from a source. For example you could use sticky notes for this or a different colour.

Once you have used all your cards, take a step back and look at the whole thing... Keep in mind that there isn't a 'right' solution, only one that best presents the research that you have done. Keep moving around cards until you are happy with what you have.

Imagine this patchwork of cards you have created is a map of your research, with each of the groups a different landmark, how would you recommend somebody navigated it? Is there an obvious order that your reader, who might not be familiar with any of this, should visit these places? You might want to add some arrows on sticky notes to remind you of this.

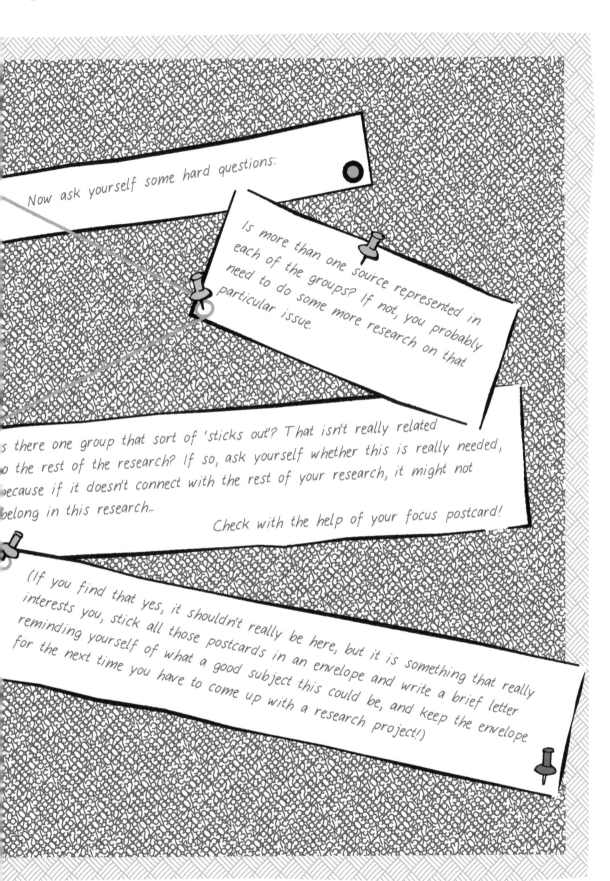

Now ask yourself some hard questions:

Is more than one source represented in each of the groups? If not, you probably need to do some more research on that particular issue.

s there one group that sort of 'sticks out'? That isn't really related o the rest of the research? If so, ask yourself whether this is really needed, because if it doesn't connect with the rest of your research, it might not belong in this research...

Check with the help of your focus postcard!

(If you find that yes, it shouldn't really be here, but it is something that really interests you, stick all those postcards in an envelope and write a brief letter reminding yourself of what a good subject this could be, and keep the envelope for the next time you have to come up with a research project!)

Use this as the basis for organising your research. (If you are working on a long research project, you might want to take pictures of it regularly so that you have a record of how it changes.)

This will become the basis of the written structure for your text.

The Initial Spillage
Drafting Content

At this point the time has come to write your first draft.

    You have thought about your focus.
    You have collected evidence.
    You have done your reading.
    You have thought about all the evidence you have found.
    You have even ordered it.
    You have done some writing along the way.

        ...it is time to write a first draft of what you have found.

And here is some good news:

this doesn't have to be perfect in any way, shape or form!

Don't worry about spelling or grammar. Don't worry about the order of your points. Just get the information that you have in your head and put it on the blank paper or screen. You will never have to show this to anybody else, so not only doesn't it need to be perfect, it doesn't even need to be good. It can be shockingly bad – that doesn't matter, **the important thing is that you write a first draft**.

Think of it as 'spilling the beans'. In a way this is an idiom used to encourage people to tell you about something, maybe to betray a confidence. And this is exactly what this draft is meaning to do, put all the information that you have on paper. The visual here also works - think of baked beans spilling out of a can: chances are it looks like a mess, but there are lots of beans in there (the bits of information that you have picked up) and they are all connected by the sauce (just like your bits of information are connected by the focus you have chosen).

In academia this spis called the 'shitty' first draft (yes, that is a thing, pretty much everybody's first draft is bad).
... and once you have done this, move on to thinking about how you can revise this first draft into making all this information presentable.

Once you have written your first (shitty) draft, you should spend some time deciding what form you will present it in.

As we have seen when looking at the secondary sources, there are many different ways in which information can be presented. These are called different **genres**.

Now if you are a student at the moment you might not really have a choice here, you might have to write an academic essay, a business report, a reflective journal or any number of specific assignments. All of these have different rules they follow in that

- There are different lengths that are appropriate;
- They are written for different audiences;
- They use different formality in writing;
- They might need visuals, like photographs or charts;
- Etc.

And the same goes for all genres – if you wanted to (or had to) write a filmscript, a fairy tale, a text message, a letter or a poem, for example, those would all follow different rules.

A good way of visualising this is by thinking about this as dressing - you can dress up your information in different ways - some of them are more appropriate than others for the audience you want to reach and the points you want to get across.

A business report, for example, could be thought of as quite formal, like a three-piece suit there are some things you need to make it work, and it could be finished off by accessories (extras that in academic terms are 'appendices', i.e. supporting information).

A tweet could be described as a mankini – small and to the point, and possibly also attention seeking!

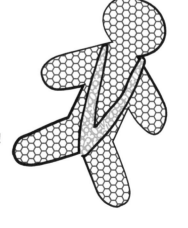

Think about the information you have and the different genres you could present this in. Pick one (or a number) and think about how these genres are like outfits - what would they be like if they were clothes and why? How would they be different from each other?

Now think about the academic essay you have to write - what do you know about this genre?

Make a list

_____

_____

_____

_____

_____

_____

_____

_____

_____

_____

Have you asked yourself the following questions...

Is there a word count?
Are there specific conventions when it comes to the language?
Is there a certain audience? Who is it?
What should the language be like?

Now design an outfit that represents the rules that you are aware of. What clothes would represent this best? something revealing? colourful? extravagant? are there accessories?

use this doll to design
your academic essay
outfit

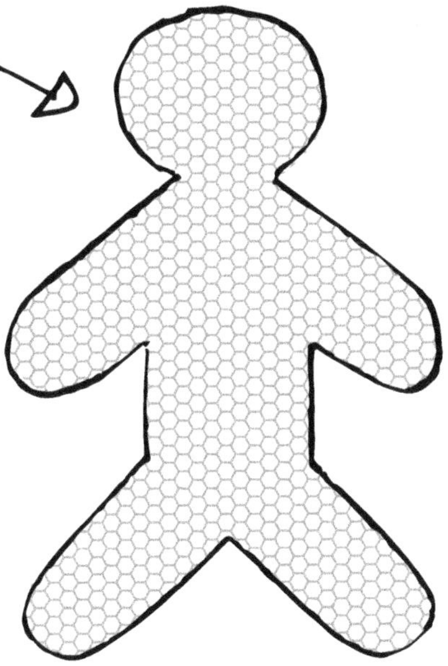

use this space to explain
why this outfit represents
an academic essay

Students that are new to academic writing often visualise an academic essay as a bit like a prison uniform:
One size fits all it seems to contain a list of black and white facts weighted down by a ball and chain of punishing academic conventions and not much fun.

When really what they should see is the potential of a well-structured garment, maybe there are some old-fashioned or traditional flourishes, like a bustle, pleats or godets - the layers that develop the information further and underpin the argument. It needs to be well-balanced, but in a more considered, intricate and structured way than the prison uniform, more like an Elizabethan gown, for example.

Depending on the level of academic study, the outfit might change. A PhD thesis, for example, is rather like an old-fashioned diving suit - able to withstand a lot of pressure, but with little flexibility as well as very focused, but with a limited field of vision.

In order to make our communication as effectively as possible, we need to consider the genre that is most appropriate to use.
Of course we need to be sure of the content - what idea we need to communicate. But we also need to ask ourselves what our audience expects and in what context our message will be presented.
Every one of these contexts has different rules, and thinking about these rules can help us 'dress up' our message in a way that will make it heard more readily.

The following describes the traditional academic essay, but what is required of you might be different! That's why it is important to identify the rules as you did on the previous spread.

The Overwater Iceberg
Structuring Essays

All the work you have done so far has been part of the 'underwater' portion of our iceberg (see page 9). These are all crucial, but little of this will be visible to your readers.
Now it is time to think a bit more about the structure of how to actually present your argument – the part of the iceberg that is showing above the waterline.

Putting together an academic essay might be a bit different to what you are used to. The trick is to think of this as your reader (remember the polar bear?) exploring the iceberg starting at the waterline and working up towards the tip of it.

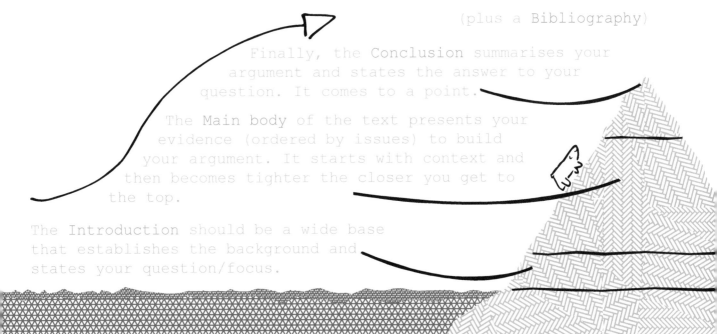

(plus a Bibliography)

Finally, the **Conclusion** summarises your argument and states the answer to your question. It comes to a point.

The **Main** body of the text presents your evidence (ordered by issues) to build your argument. It starts with context and then becomes tighter the closer you get to the top.

The **Introduction** should be a wide base that establishes the background and states your question/focus.

The introduction/main body/conclusion structure sometimes can stump people who are not familiar with it, because mainly you are expected to include the same information in them, only with a different level of detail! A good way of dealing with this is writing the middle bit first, and then putting together the introduction and conclusion afterwards.

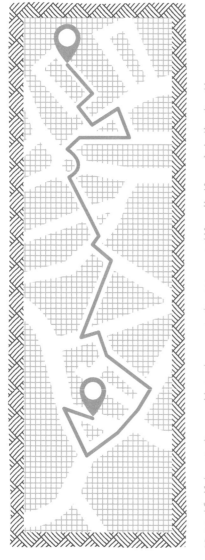

Now if this main section is your journey, with all the details in it, almost like taking snapshots along the way, you need to begin it with an introduction. This should describe to your reader where this journey will lead – and how you are going to get there. Like planning the journey on a map, this doesn't include too many details; it just gives an overall view of where you are headed and how you are going to end up there. So write this up, clearly stating the question you want to answer (even if the question is in your title! Your focus postcard should help you with this), maybe giving a bit of background (why are you taking this particular journey?), and the main 'landmarks' you will be dealing with – remember all the issues you clustered together on your pinboard? This is the time to mention those.

Remember when we were talking about the differences in looking at a map and taking an actual walk along the street noticing things? This is something that can be useful here, too. Your Patchwork Pinboard is already a map of sorts. Now you have to decide in what order to take your reader through this. Just like planning a journey, you need to think about which bits are close to another, what needs to come before something else. Putting this 'journey' on paper in a linear way will become your main body of the text. (A good way of doing this is once you have decided on your order, take the cards on the pinboard and change them into a line, effectively making a storyboard, like if you were planning a movie. This is the order in which you should write up your argument.)

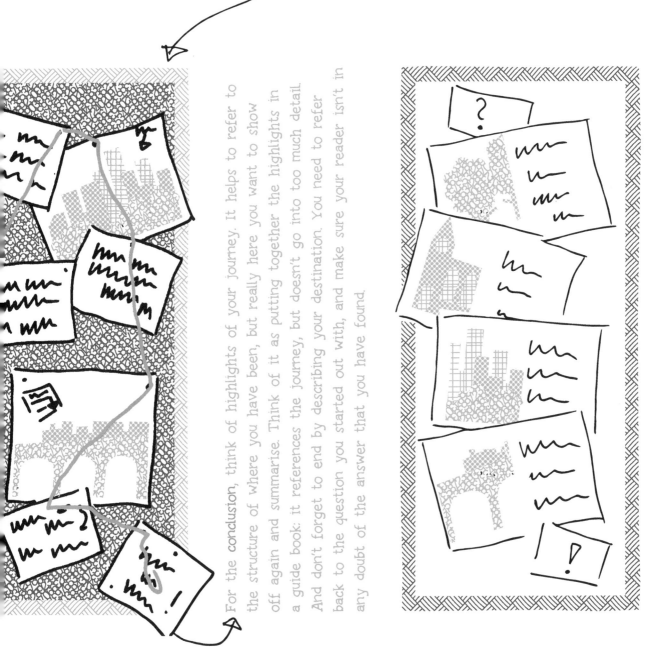

For the conclusion, think of highlights of your journey. It helps to refer to the structure of where you have been, but really here you want to show off again and summarise. Think of it as putting together the highlights in a guide book: it references the journey, but doesn't go into too much detail. And don't forget to end by describing your destination. You need to refer back to the question you started out with, and make sure your reader isn't in any doubt of the answer that you have found.

Use the FIRST DRAFT you have already written as the MAIN BODY OF YOUR TEXT. Use your PATCHWORK PINBOARD to help you figure out whether you have put the information in the right order - and to add an INTRODUCTION to the beginning and a CONCLUSION to the end.

We have already talked about the importance of finding good sources at an appropriate level and referencing them. An academic research essay needs to be evidence based and a good way to present evidence is by not just **referring** to other people's work

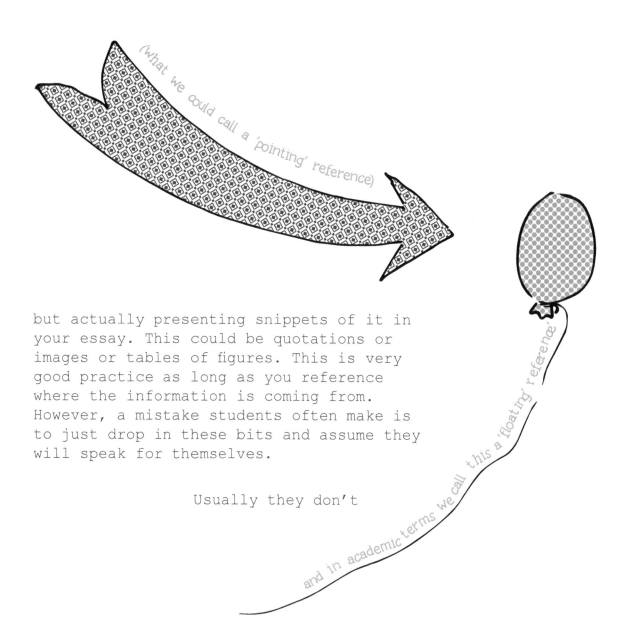

(what we could call a 'pointing' reference)

but actually presenting snippets of it in your essay. This could be quotations or images or tables of figures. This is very good practice as long as you reference where the information is coming from. However, a mistake students often make is to just drop in these bits and assume they will speak for themselves.

Usually they don't

and in academic terms we call this a 'floating' reference'

What you should do is think of your evidence like the main attraction of a sandwich:

the filling!

The idea behind a sandwich is that you use the bread as a sort of encasement to allow you to eat the filling more easily.

A piece of evidence is similar, you need to encase it with contextual information that will make it easier for your reader to understand and digest.

Embedding Evidence

It is helpful to introduce your evidence.

This is like the top bread slice of your sandwich.

Here you tell your reader what this evidence is and where it comes from, mention the original author and possibly the source (and type of source) it is from.

Your evidence itself is, of course, the star - so this could be seen as the filling of your sandwich. But make sure that you don't leave it too big, you want something that your readers can get their teeth into, but not something they will choke on.

This is why it is also important to follow up your evidence with an explanation -

with the bottom slice of your bread.

This is incredibly important because it allows you to make the link between the evidence and your argument, to guide your readers toward the details you want them to notice and the analysis of the evidence that you are putting forward. This is also why it is so important to refer to images in the text, because you need to explain them. An image you don't refer to is lost to the argument and becomes little more than pretty illustration, no matter how relevant it is.

While you can leave out the introduction (to make it an open sandwich so to speak), you should never leave out the explanation of what the data you use as evidence means in the context of your argument.

Go through your draft and highlight the evidence you use in two different colours: one for pointing references and one for actual evidence included (a quotation or an image, or any raw piece of data) - for images don't highlight the image itself, but rather where you mention it in the text).

Then, using two more colours, highlight introductory information to that evidence and finally your explanation and interpretation of it.

Check that every piece of evidence has at least one bit of explanation attached. Also check how much direct evidence you have -   think bite-size bits rather than a whole meal...

By now your essay should be in pretty good shape. You should have collected a lot of research from good academic sources, but formed this into your own text by only using the information that stays focused and allows you to present a balanced argument.

You should have found out about the referencing system you are supposed to use, and included in-text citations for the information you are using, as well as have a bibliography with all the references you have used.

You should have organised your information into

> an introduction,
> a main body and
> a conclusion.

You should have checked your quotations, making sure that they are properly embedded and not floating.

The Icing on the Cake
Formalising Language

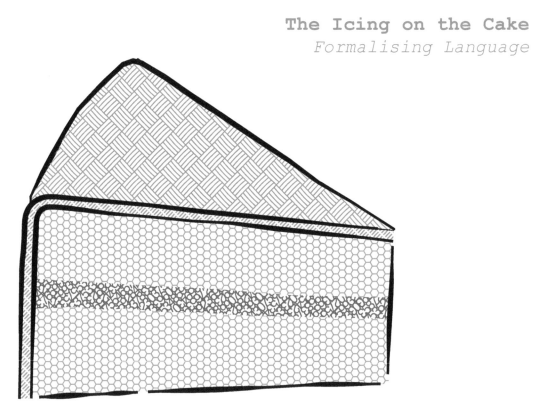

The last thing you need to do is to check the formalities. Making your writing sound formal is a bit like the icing on the cake - it polishes your piece of research off nicely, but in relation to the other stages, you don't want to spend too much time on it. It is much better to have a decent chunk of cake that is nicely baked, than a really thin piece of underbaked cake that comes with loads of icing and looks beautiful but is pretty much inedible.
Depending on the discipline you write in (and possibly the tutor you have), the level of how formal you are expected to write will be different. So this is something you need to find out.

Here are some things to consider:

Personal Pronouns. Some tutors will not let you use 'I' or 'we'. There's a reason for that - if you can write an essay without personal pronouns you are much more likely to base it on evidence rather than on your personal feelings. So find out what the policy on personal pronouns is.

If you are not allowed to use them, go through your draft and highlight all of them. Go through each case and ask yourself how you know what you are stating and where the evidence is coming from. Very often sentences with 'I' can be replaced by references to the evidence: instead of telling your reader that you think something, tell them why something is that way.

Contractions. You shouldn't really use contractions (so if this was an academic essay, this sentence would be "You should not use contractions" - funny how suddenly the 'really' sounds weird, too).

Go through the essay and replace all of them.

Technical Terms. Your audience is most likely an interested non-expert. This means that you need to define technical terms, either the first time you use them in the text, or in a footnote, or - if you have a lot of them - you might want to include a glossary (a list of all the technical terms and their definitions).

Go through your essay and make sure that all the technical terms are explained properly.

Beware of the Thesaurus. Yes, a thesaurus is a handy thing to have, if you want to sound more academic, but never ever use a word in your writing when you are not completely sure of what it means. It is better to write in plain English than trying to sound academic, but getting it wrong.

Colloquialisms. On the other hand, you also should avoid sounding like you are just talking to your mates in the pub. Think about more formal ways of expressing yourself, and never use txt speak in an essay (unless it is about texting and you are giving examples).

Go through your text and make sure that you understand all the words you are using, and that it doesn't sound too informal.

The Review Continuum
Proofreading Text

Now that you have gone through your essay multiple times, refining it every time, leave it for a while (if possible). Taking a break from it will give you a fresh eye.

Once you have done this, you should **proofread** it again.

Spellcheck. Use the spellchecker that comes with your word processing software. It probably won't pick up all your spelling mistakes, but it will catch some of them.

Read it out. Reading it out loud can help you spot problems with both grammar and spelling.

Get a second opinion. Give it to somebody else to read to see if it makes sense, or if they can find any spelling mistakes. Ideally give it to both somebody who knows about the field you are writing in, and to somebody who doesn't.

Make changes based on the feedback you have gotten.

Avoid Sweeping Statements. Showing your work to somebody outside of your field can help you identify sweeping statements. You need to be very careful not to use generalisations in your essay, no matter how 'obvious' things appear to you they might not be to anyone else. Rather, be specific – exactly who and what are you talking about? – and when in doubt show off the evidence you have found in order to define your terms properly.

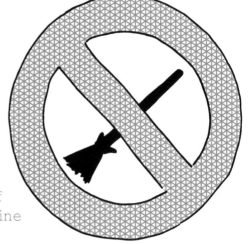

Define your Terms. Also make sure that you carefully define how you are using special terms, like theories, for example. Not everybody uses these in the same way, and when in doubt, explain clearly how you are using them. The same goes for the context – have you explained in the introduction what specific context you are looking at? That could be a particular period in time, for example, or a specific region.

Make changes to clearly define your terms and context.

Referencing.

Double check that you have followed the referencing system you need to,
both in the text and in your bibliography.

After that last round of review (and you responding to any issues that have come up), all that is left is to make it ready for hand-in. Check whether your tutor wants it to be presented in a certain way (font, point size, line spacing, how to do captions for images, margins, etc.) and try to follow these guidelines as closely as possible.

And then hand it in.

For more tips and tricks when it comes to essay writing, go to
http://writingbypictures.wordpress.com

Really use feedback you
get from your teachers to
improve future work. If you
don't act on it and apply
it to your next piece of
writing both getting and
giving feedback becomes a
waste of time.

So, go through each essay
feedback you get and make
sure you understand it
all - teachers don't mind
if you come back to them
to clarify things. Then
think about how you could
improve on the weaknesses
that the feedback shows -
for example: Do you need to
check how the referencing
system you are supposed to
use works? Do you need to
work on the structure of
the essay? Do you need to
be more careful with your
proofreading? Act on these
questions to make your
writing better the next
time round -
and particularly use them
before you hand in the next
one.

Printed in the USA
CPSIA information can be obtained
at www.ICGtesting.com
LVHW072311290923
759529LV00017B/856

9 780957 665224